THE GATHERING OF
THE ELDERS AND OTHER POEMS

THE GATHERING OF THE ELDERS AND OTHER POEMS

Wesli Court

The Gathering of the Elders
by Wesli Court

© 2010 by Lewis Turco

Cover design: Trisha Hadley

All rights reserved. No part of this book may be used or reproduced in any manner whatsoever without written permission from the publisher, except in the case of brief quotations embodied in articles and reviews.

Published by

-Star Cloud Press®-
6137 East Mescal Street
Scottsdale, Arizona 85254-5418

ISBN:

978-1-932842-43-2 (paper) — $ 14.95

Library of Congress Control Number: 2010928673

Printed in the United States of America

OTHER BOOKS BY THE AUTHOR

The Collected Lyrics of Lewis Turco / Wesli Court, 1953-2004

The Airs of Wales, 1981

Curses and Laments, 1978

Murgatroyd and Mabel, 1978

Courses in Lambents: Poems, 1977

DEDICATION

This book is dedicated to the memory
of all those who have left us

ACKNOWLEDGMENTS

The author owes thanks for, and acknowledgment of, first publication to the editors and publishers of these print and on-line venues: *The Blue Moon Review* and *The Syracuse New Times* for simultaneous publication of "Blues for George Gershwin" and to a web reprint in *Gershwin Discussion Forum*; *Confrontation* for "Letter to Mother"; *The Davidson Miscellany* for "Our Hero" and "Letter to an Editor"; *The Formalist* for "Avatars," "Elegy on Eight Lines by Conrad Aiken," "The Gathering of the Elders," "Herb Plays with the Blues," "Letter to a Drowned Boy" (reprinted in *The Evansville Review*); "The Shadowman," and "The Winter's Falls" (reprinted in *Rhyming Poems: A Contemporary Anthology*, edited by William Baer, University of Evansville Press, 2007); *From East to West: Bicoastal Verse* for "Columbian Ode" (reprinted in *Trellis Magazine*) and "Sestina" (reprinted in *A Poet's Ear: A Handbook of Meter and Form*, edited by Annie Finch, Ann Arbor: University of Michigan Press, 2010); *The Hampden-Sydney Poetry Review* for "Distant Sound," "On a Word by Katherine Mansfield," "Seasons Down East," "A Cautionary Poem," "Another Cautionary Poem," and "Yet Another Cautionary Poem"; *Hellas* for "The Birdsong Blues"; *Italian Americana* for "Slumber" and "The Falcon Carol"; *Kansas Quarterly* for "Letter to a Hall-of-Famer"; *Measure* for "After School"; *New CollAge* for "The Obsession" (reprinted in *Patterns of Poetry*, edited by Miller Williams, Baton Rouge: Louisiana State University Press, 1986; *An Exaltation of Forms, Contemporary Poets Celebrate the Diversity of Their Art*, edited by Annie Finch and Kathrine Varnes, Ann Arbor: University of Michigan Press, 2002, and in *The Practice of Creative Writing*, edited by Heather Sellers, New York: Bedford/St. Martin, 2007); *New Virginia Review* for "Letter to a Grandsire"; *Northern New England Review* for "Letter to a Baritone" and "Letter to a Gardener"; *Off the Coast* for "Stile"; *Orbis* (United Kingdom) for "Letter to a Three-Year-Old"; *Per Contra* for "Bloomsday," "Passing the Time," "Second Sight" (the second part of "Double Vision"), and "Yeats' Birthday"; *Per Contra Light Verse Supplement 2009* for "Our Little Span" and "The Universal Leaf"; *Poetry Porch* for "A Paternal Curse" and "The Shade"; *Sparrow* for "The View from a Winter Garret"; *Sonnetto Poesia* (Canada) for "Winter Blinds";

Spring: The Journal of the E. E.; Cummings Society for "Lines To Be Etched on a Window"; *Timothy McSweeney's Internet Tendency, Sestinas*, for "Tsunami" and "The Vision" (the first part of "Double Vision"); *The Tower Journal* for "The Dame Who Carried Her Cane in Her Coffin" and "Sweet Jean"; *Trellis Magazine* for "The Black Death," and *Voices in Italian Americana* for "Slumber" and "The Stairwell."

"Reflections in an Attic Room" originally appeared in its entirety in *Patterns of Poetry*, edited by Miller Williams, Baton Rouge: Louisiana State University Press, 1986.

"The Boneyard Blues" was originally published as part of an essay, "Black Poetry," in *Visions and Revisions of American Poetry* by Lewis Turco, Fayetteville: University of Arkansas Press, 1986.

"About the Young" was originally published in *Scarecrow Poetry*, edited by Robert McGovern and Stephen Haven, Ashland: Ashland Poetry Press, 1994.

"The Great Ice Storm of '98" first appeared in *And What Rough Beast, Poems at the End of the Century*, edited by Robert McGovern and Stephen Haven, Ashland: Ashland Poetry Press, 1999.

"Envoi," "The Obsession," and "Reflections in an Attic Room" appeared in *The Book of Forms: A Handbook of Poetics*, Third Edition, by Lewis Turco, Lebanon, NH: University Press of New England, 2000.

"The Night Before the Battle" appeared originally in *Voices in the Gallery: Writers on Art*, edited by Grant Holcomb, Rochester: University of Rochester Press, 2001.

"The Premonition" was first published in *Poetry: A Pocket Anthology*, edited by R. S. Gwynn, New York: Penguin Academics, 2006.

Table of Contents

SONGS AND SONNETS

The Gathering of the Elders	1
Year by Year	3
The Universal Leaf	5
Our Little Span	6
Avatars	7
About the Young	8
On a Word by Katherine Mansfield	9
The Shade	10
The Stairwell	11
The View from a Winter Garret	12
Winter Blinds	13
The Winter's Falls	14
The Premonition	15
The Shadowman	16
The Falcon Carol	18

EPISTLES AND MONOLOGUES

Letters to the Dead

Our Hero	21
Letters to Two Children Drowned:	
Letter to a Drowned Boy	23
Letter to a Three-Year-Old	25
Letter to a Grandsire	26
Letter to a Baritone	28
Letter to a Gardener	30
Letter to a Hall-of-Famer	31
Letter to an Editor	33
Slumber	35
The Obsession	37

Reflections in an Attic Room 39
Letter to Mother 54
The Dead Letter Office 56

ODES AND ELEGIES

The Birdsong Blues 61
The Dame Who Carried Her Cane in Her Coffin 62
Elegy on Eight Lines by Conrad Aiken 64
The Black Death 66
The Night Before the Battle 67
Blues for George Gershwin 69
Distant Sound 71
The Great Ice Storm of Ninety-Eight 72
Herb Plays with the Blues 73
After School 75
The Day We Bombed the Moon 77
Columbian Ode 79
Lines To Be Etched on a Window 81
Tsunami 82
Russet Oak 84
Yeats' Birthday 85
Seasons Down East 86

CAUTIONARY POEMS

Fathers 91
A Paternal Curse 93
Passing the Time 94
Double Vision: A Double Sestina 95
Sestina 98
A Cautionary Poem 100
Another Cautionary Poem 101
Yet Another Cautionary Poem 102

Bloomsday	103
Fond Poem	104
Currency: A Sonnenizio	105
Stile	106
Sweet Jean	107

EPILOGUE

The Boneyard Blues	111
Envoi	114

SONGS AND SONNETS

THE GATHERING OF THE ELDERS

Here we are gathered at this node in time
Listening to the stillness in our veins,
Hearing the frost riming the windowpanes
With sounds that sound like age — the age-old sounds
Of clockwork hands making their ancient rounds,
The siling sands whispering their grains
Through the narrow arteries of glass
That weigh upon our mantels, weigh and pass
From substance into shadow. Here we are,
Participating in our golden age
By tapping on these keys to find a rhyme
Perhaps for melancholy or for rage,
For snowfall drifting slowly through the rare
December wind, falling upon the page
Like letters of some runic alphabet
Shaped like stars. But what's the point of this
Synod of the elders gathered here
To listen to very little — the subtle hiss
Of a bit of sleet falling down the flue
To kiss the fire and in that mating turn
To mist that dissipates as if on cue
Back into the thinnest air? We sit and burn
For what is lost, for what we cannot get
As if we ever wanted it at all,
As if we don't, as if we couldn't care
More or less for everything. We tap
Upon our keys and make the runes perform
A bit of wintry magic just to prove

It hasn't been a waste of time, remove
All doubt about the drift of all we've done
Before the sands run out, before the sap
Turns into the amber that traps everyone.

YEAR BY YEAR

When we are born we have no clue
Why we are here, what we should do,
Therefore we flail about and yell
Till we are changed or held and fed,
And then at last, when all is well,
We take the world into our head,
Into our hands, until our fear
Begins to wane and disappear.

We enter school and learn to read
And how to cope with every need
That rises out of books and play.
We learn to cope with those around us
With whom we interact each day,
With all the people who surround us.
As we grow older year by year
Our playmates start to disappear.

Then we enter adolescence
To discover that the essence
Of existence seems hormonal:
We must learn to deal with excess
Of enticements pheremonal,
With the battle of the sexes.
As we grow older year by year
Our girl and boy friends disappear.

When finally we come of age
We take our place upon the stage
Of life and do what adults do:
Choose a career and graduate,
Settle on a friend or two,
Begin to think about a mate.
So we mature a bit each year,
And see our lovers disappear.

We settle down and get a house
Or an apartment with a spouse
Or live-in. Then the kids arrive
To take our energy and time —
No matter what, they seem to thrive.
We do as well, we're in our prime
Until there comes that primal year
When all our children disappear.

The two of us are left alone
And then, perhaps, there's only one
Because what else is there to do
Except look back and try to find
The future that we barely knew
Before it started to unwind
And we grew older, year by year,
Watching our elders disappear?

Now here we are. The moon turns blue
No longer and the days are few
When we have anything of note
To celebrate or fill our minds.
We have no projects to promote
Or interests of different kinds,
For we've grown older year by year
And seen our lifetime disappear.

THE UNIVERSAL LEAF

The universe requires that we be born.
As soon as that's been done, it's out to get us.
We become Peter Rabbit in the lettuce
Trying to hide away from Farmer Brown.
Hopelessly we hope we won't be torn
Away, apart. We pray he will forget us,
That he will have some pity once he's met us,
But all such self-delusion is forlorn.

Our hopes and dreams must come at last to grief
If they're not wrecked already, partway through
This span of years. We're well aware that worse
Must come to worst. We cower beneath this leaf
Which we turn over to find what we always knew:
No one cares. Not even the universe.

OUR LITTLE SPAN

We live our little span of years and make
The things we can — an elegy, a mote,
A play or dialogue, a dance or note
Sung in a minor key. We undertake
To quench a thirst that nothing else can slake
This side of Paradise. We wear the coat
Of many colors; in the zephyrs float
The flags of all the dreams we must forsake,

For there is little else that we may do
To pass the time besides wear out our minds
And bodies in the everyday of toil.
We plant the seed in the everlasting soil
And watch it blossom in its several kinds
Until the field lies fallow in the dew.

AVATARS
For Miller Williams, on his retirement

It's time to start to think of growing old.
We've put it off as long as is feasible,
Perhaps. When one is young, the impossible
Is what one sings of: love and death, the bold
Clasp of the ideal mistress and the cold
Grasp of the grave: romantic cock-and-bull.
One seldom writes of the Unspeakable
Although its avatars are manifold.

So now it's time to think of what we see
Staring at us over the bathroom sink
Each morning. Here's the fellow we've defied
All our lifetime long. We perfectly
Discern the Shadowman beyond the wink
Of hours in the glass. We cannot hide.

ABOUT THE YOUNG

The world is all about the young;
   We elders are wrung out of it
Though we continue here among
The relevant. The clock has rung
   One chime too often. Our phlegm and spit

Are all the juices we have left —
   What would we do with more than these?
Our bedward turns are less than deft
These nights, our winding sheets bereft
   Of art. There are no mysteries.

Then what's the point? The future's all,
   And when there's none, or very little,
We hang our portraits on the wall
And walk away from hall to hall
   To find a place to sit and whittle

Away our last few hacking days
   And piddle away our aching nights.
The world is all about the ways
The young make young and not the grays
   That color our brows with northern lights.

But looking back at all the mess,
   The scrabble, the lyrics badly sung
To music composed in wild distress,
One shakes one's head and mutters, "Yes,
   The world *is* all about the young."

ON A WORD BY KATHERINE MANSFIELD

Along the beach the lady wearing white
Makes her shell-like way, the spray kissing
Her knees. We nearly hear the fish whispering
about her in the waves. She walks, but might

Have ridden seahorses promenading
Had she wished. She is a lady of fashion,
High-waisted, well made. The sun is crystalline
Upon her parasol. Her gown flouncing,

All her appointments minutely kept, she glances
Among the emerald waves, and as she strolls,
The susurrus of the fawning ocean rolls
After her. She flirts, she blushes, dances

And titters for her lovers. She sighs, "My dear!
It's hot beneath this perishall, I fear."

THE SHADE

How could I know that such a thing exists?
Although the bathroom seemed extremely cold,
I couldn't know the boy had slit his wrists

and bled to death in the bath. No one had told
the story to me, for I was a visitor.
Although the bathroom seemed extremely cold,

I had to use it. I'd stand in the corridor
and stretch to switch the light on, then slide in
shivering, for I was a visitor

in Louisville that winter. I'd glide in
as though on a sheet of ice, do what I must,
then stretch to switch the light off. I'd slide in

and out as fast as possible, adjust
to a shade I never saw, that was always there,
as though on a sheet of ice. Do what I must,

I did, and told my friends. I saw them stare —
they'd known about the shade that was always there!
How could *I* know that such a thing exists?
I hadn't known the boy had slit his wrists.

THE STAIRWELL

The hall is empty for a little while.
Visions bloom behind our eyes; our dread
Becomes the future. The bathroom suicide
Leaves cold silence lying on the tile.

Who are these phantoms whom we try to keep
Alive in dream? This is the life they know
Above the gravel. They cannot have it, though
They will not be outcast. We ring them up

And ask, "What's new? Have you found your calling?"
Their smiles are wan upon the dawn's chiming.
We wave farewell again, continue rhyming
Well away upon the stairwell falling

Beneath our feet. We find that they have fled,
Leaving behind their stillness on the tread.

THE VIEW FROM A WINTER GARRET

Skies are gray and winter is settling down
Past my attic window as I write.
I see my neighbors' roofs adrift through town
Blown by the wind winding them in white.

The current of my mind begins to spill
Into a fault of time. I watch a flight
Of gulls come rising out of chimneys, fill
A fold of sky that falls in siftings there

Into Ontario below the hill.
I hear the wind build palaces of air
And ice along the shore of Whitman's lake.
Only silence will make a dwelling where

Music must turn to crystal to survive,
And seagulls scull like snowfall come alive.

WINTER BLINDS

The winter evening lies beyond my blinds
Waiting for me to listen to its lies.
Why should I do so? It merely falsifies
The bitter wind whining at what it finds
Lying behind my glass. It takes all kinds
Of dusks to make November. The evening tries
To scratch the pane with air, with the stuff of sighs —
A skein of tales and yarns, but it unwinds

And lies there breathing hard. How may one dare
To tell the truth, lie in the night with eyes
And ears wide open, hearing the pantomime,
Seeing the shadow world of passing time?
To do so may be daring but not wise.
Best wind a skein of rime around despair.

THE WINTER'S FALLS

The winter moon stands against the night
Over the falls, spinning its silver line
Down the gorge, illuminating the white

Fields to either side of the icy spine
That holds the scene together. The couple pose
Upon the bridge. They speak in crystalline

Silhouette — their lips do not disclose
The sound of syllables being whipped away
Into the spruces on the banks. Suppose

That they have nothing at all they want to say.
Imagine it's all been said, that words are a sleight
Of sunlight uttered idly during the day.

Perhaps we are not here to say a thing,
Only to listen to the full moon sing.

THE PREMONITION

The first two planes had crashed. I'd known they would
as I watched AirOps from the Gunner's Bridge,
and I'd seen everything from where I stood.
The wings folded along the fuselage
on this new day relieved me. I was glad,
as I watched AirOps from the Gunner's Bridge,
that this third time there would be nothing bad
about to happen. My instincts had been wrong
on this new day. I was deeply glad
this pilot would be safe. I looked along
the deck as the plane was parked, then looked away
before it happened — my gut had not been wrong!
The jet had not cut out! I saw it sway,
then disappear over the *Hornet's* side
near where it had been parked. I looked away —
At least the first two pilots hadn't died!
Those first two planes had crashed. I'd known they would,
but this one fell along the *Hornet's* side,
and I'd seen everything from where I stood.

THE SHADOWMAN

This is the year when everybody died —
This is the year when friends and neighbors died,
Took that short trip or ended the long slide.

Jim shot himself on Cemetery Road,
Left an ironic note beside the road.
No one heard his desperate heart explode.

Our frightened former next-door neighbor went —
Rita, the fearful widow from next-door went
To join her husband John in the firmament.

Paul's heart quit because his cough would not.
His life went up in smoke, for he could not
Stop puffing soon enough — so he would trot

Along our streets slower than folks could walk,
Jog the streets slower than we could walk
And slower than the shadowman can stalk.

Cooper's blood sluggishly turned to whey
In his pale veins — slowly turned to whey
Beneath the translucent skin now turned to clay.

Kermit and Dorothy lost this chilly spring
To the sickle and the crab — lost the spring
To the dim weather and the scorpion's sting.

And Mag, our neighbor on the other side,
Next door toward the lake on our north side,
Father of my son's best friend, has died

Because he loved his beer more than his life,
Loved his suds more than his very life,
Let alone his daughter, his son, his wife.

The shadowman comes tapping down the street,
His feet come stuttering along the street.
Nobodaddy's patrolling, walking his beat.

Hear him, townsmen, between the curbs of night,
Among our yards, towing the craft of night
Whether the hour is dusky or dark or light.

Listen to him breathing in the walls
Of all our houses, breathing in the walls,
In our kitchens and in the empty halls;

Stop when you listen and whisper to the dust,
"These are the names of neighbors scrawled in dust,
Whistled to shadow, scattered in a gust."

THE FALCON CAROL

Upon the currents of air the raptors fly,
Upon the soaring updrafts the raptors fly —
The call of winter is the falcon's cry.

Upon the plain the beasts of burden lie,
Out on the grassland the beasts of burden lie.
The secret snow falls out of the silent sky

Onto an inn, a stable and a sty,
Onto the stable standing beside a sty.
The call of winter is the falcon's cry.

The star stands shining like a glittering eye
Above the stable, gleams like a glittering eye
While secret snow falls out of the silent sky.

The call of winter is the falcon's cry.
The secret snow falls out of the silent sky.

EPISTLES AND MONOLOGUES

LETTERS TO THE DEAD
In Memory of Luigi and May, John and Bertha

OUR HERO

Here is our Hero, opening his eyes.
The daylight rises like a welling tide
And floats him out of slumber into time.
Two eggs and toast; coffee in a cup
Of thermal plastic; the thermostat turned up.
Slowly blood and temperature rise.

Shower and shave, and then his socks and pants
Crawl up his flesh to lock his shirt-tail in,
Though waking is his habit, and the sun
Clothes him like armor forged against those dreams
He's left among the linens — so it seems,
Or so he hopes. At least he has a chance

To down the darkness, drown it in the dawn.
For he is of an age when sleep comes hard,
But when it comes there trails behind its edge
A specter host, a horde of attic shades
Risen from the Nether Regions' glades
To walk again upon a morning lawn.

He'd buried them upstairs in trunks and cartons,
Their eyelids weighted down with trash and lace,
Mathoms and mementos: every face
Lies in its album while the hornet croons
Among the rafters summer afternoons
Or as, in spring, the maples fill with martins,

With greening leaves that fall to earth in fall —
But worst in winter. Then the photographs
Give up the ghost to cold, the petty griefs
Of dust as chill as snow. Their images
Arise, and then descend like salvages
Of musty seasons to our Hero's hall.

They walk the paisley carpet as the night
Fills with the moon. They pause before his door.
They enter, cast their shadows on the floor,
Loom over him. Then, one by one, they slide
Into his sleep — he recollects the stride
Of one, another's stance, their darkness bright

As candles guttering. The dreamer's lake
Has swallowed him — nevertheless, he sees,
His lids like film. The phantoms do not speak,
Nor does he speak to them, but words in spate
Sluice through his mind. He tries to close the gate
To capture them. He struggles to awake....

Here is our Hero, born to second sight.
The daylight rises like a welling tide
And floats him out of slumber into time...,
Two eggs and toast; coffee in a cup
Of thermal plastic; the thermostat turned up.
He takes a pad and pen and starts to write.

Two Epistles to Children Drowned:

LETTER TO A DROWNED BOY

He wants to write a letter to the child,
The boy drowned on the beach when he was young,
A boy himself. The letter is overdue.
Dear Friend, *he writes.* I recall your body flung
To that Wisconsin beach. Your flesh was blue,
A pallid blue. The day was dark, but mild —

Or was it dark? If so, why would my mother
Have taken us to swim where you had drowned?
What kind of darkness was it, has it been
Since first I saw you there where you'd been downed
By death, the first death I had ever seen?
Why had she let me see you? Did my brother

See you also? I have never asked,
But he was there, seven when I was twelve.
The firemen pumped you out. Their motor churned,
But darkness stalked that beach and, in its stealth,
Stole the march on all of us. I turned
Into a mortal. I saw that life was masked,

And underneath the mask I saw the bone.
I saw your chest sucked inward, then forced out;
I saw the blot of water on the sand
Under the hose. I saw you were without
The thing that made you you. Time waved its wand
Over the water — we blinked, and you were gone.

I don't remember feeling. I was cold.
I must have forced myself to turn to stone.
I think the crowd was small — a weekday crowd —
but since then you and I have been alone.
The Pulmotor drones, but silences are loud;
You took my hand; I cannot break your hold.

Your stillnesses encroach a ripple more
Each hour upon my sands, this beach-head birth
Allotted us, that now erodes away
Until I feel dark water sucking earth
From underfoot. The motor sings. The day
Fills my lungs. My ears begin to roar.

LETTER TO A THREE-YEAR-OLD

Ontario was calm that afternoon,
Still as the photograph of a summer day.
The beach was a fall of stones sloping down
To the water's edge. It was no day to drown,
The sun in the sky like a hazy red balloon.
Your father had been watching you at play

In depths that reached your waist and touched his knees.
The other picnickers sat on the shore
Or waded lazily not far away,
Watching you and the other children play.
The sailboats on the lake moved by degrees
Almost too small to note. One might ignore,

On such an afternoon, the shadow on
The imperceptible swell — the scudding cloud
That threw its umbra there, casting color
Along the lakeside. One might well ignore
The picnickers, the children in the sun,
The hazy heat that settled like a shroud

Impalpably on the water. Then,
Without a word or sign, summer faltered.
The silence you became still echoes loud
Upon Ontario's stones, under the shroud
Of haze and scudding cirrus. We hear it often.
The quality of stillness has been altered.

LETTER TO A GRANDSIRE

Dear Grandpa,
      Here I am at forty-five,
And you've been dead for years. When I was twelve
I came to visit you at great remove
From my home town. I caught you by the barn,
Committing an act of nature, but reproof
Was lost on you. You turned as though to warn

The empty stalls of danger. Tall and thin,
Thereafter you left the room when I came in —
You imitated smoke. I'd see you there
Beside the iron stove; you'd start, a look
Like prey upon your eyes, then disappear.
You never held a job or read a book

Your whole life long, I've heard my mother claim.
You sired nine before time quenched your flame —
Or, much more likely, grandma's. Six were sons.
They all grew up inside that shell of boards
You called a house. The sunny, windy seasons
Belabored it. The autumn fell in cords,

And you were sapped by spring, became a ghost
Who fled from grandsons, that unruly host
Sprung from your loins. You opened up your fly
And soaked the barn. You saw me watching you,
Then turned and faded off. Was it my eye,
My look of accusation? I guess you knew

That in your daughter's world, therefore in mine,
Such things did not occur. You were a swine
Cast before pearls. I blush as I remember,
Not your simple act, but my disdain.
Grandpa, I cherish that familiar member,
That glimpse of greatness, your prolific reign.

LETTER TO A BARITONE

Our Hero is remembering his friend
From second grade and high school. He recalls
The early days — on weekends they'd pretend
That they were pilots in The War. The walls
Fade out about him in his reverie,
Fade into the quartet's close harmony.

Dear Curt (*he writes*), How long have you been dead?
I don't remember. Last weekend I went back
To visit our home town. A passing dread
Lies waiting when we double in our track,
But this time I picked up the telephone
And called our choral teacher. Pure cornpone,

I know, but hearing him I felt relieved —
He sounded as he used to. I had brunch
Next day at his house — hard to be believed,
But he was just the same. I'd played a hunch
and won this once. We spent a splendid day;
We quipped and talked, and then I walked away.

He had our pictures, Curt, down in his den
Upon his desk, and on the wall as well:
That barbershop cartoon that I'd forgotten,
Drawn by our tenor but signed by one and all.
He tried to give it to me; I demurred.
I couldn't take it, but I nearly heard

Those chords again, spellbinding when we blended
Into a single voice of chiming parts;
The ringing silence when the song was ended —
This pen pursues its way by fits and starts.
"How maudlin this would sound to anyone,"
I think at first; then, "Lord, we did have fun."

The ringing silence when the song was ended:
No doubt that's what we've heard since you've been gone.
Tony and Ed became what they intended,
And so did I. We work, we mow the lawn,
Drive the kids to the dentist, wives to the store,
But we never get together anymore.

LETTER TO A GARDENER

Uncle Alfred, skinny as a pole,
Deaf as any post, blind as a vole,
You felt your way through age along the rows
And hillocks of your garden, furbelows
And furrows. Maine potatoes were your eyes,
And corn, your ears to hear the grackles' cries.

You felt your way through age along the rows —
You laid the autumn straitly in windrows
After your harvest, green and gold and brown,
Peered out of Mason jars all over town.
Your labors rested with us winter-long;
Now I will pay you for them with a song.

After your harvest, green and gold and brown,
I helped to bear your burden, Alfred, down
At last to harvest home. It was as light
To me as sun by day or dew by night,
Uncle Alfred, skinny as a pole,
Deaf as any post, blind as a vole.

LETTER TO A HALL-OF-FAMER

Our Hero reminisces, half awake.
The radio is playing, and his cat,
Black as midnight, is making up to him.
He wants to write a letter for the sake
Of auld lang syne; however, he must trim,
First, thirty years and more from all those that

He has accrued. He must remember when
The summer morning broke across a street
Of elms and maples. Mr. Walsh, *he writes,*
I couldn't have been more than nine or ten.
I slumbered soundly through such dreamless nights,
And rose up early, anxious to compete

With time, discover which of us should last
And which succumb. None of my friends had risen;
The street was mine — until I saw your pickup
Before the enigmatic shack we passed
Each day that we played ball. We used to kick up
Dust in the lot beside the shack. A dozen

Times when we had started home that summer,
We'd stopped before the dusty window panes,
Cupped our hands and tried to peer inside.
We thought we saw machines. We lived on rumor —
When we thought of it. Our interest died.
And then I saw your truck, all dents and stains,

Parked at the curb that dewy summer morning.
I found you bottling milk with your machines,
Racking bottles. You were a quiet man,
So tall that, as you loaded up, the awning
Brushed your head. So that's how they began,
Those early hours filled with brilliant greens

Along the bumpy roads outside of town
Where you were hailed as "Mr. Walsh" or "Ed"
By customers who met us at the door.
The milk was winter white — it wore a crown
Of cream beneath the cap. Those mornings wore
A luster. Your obituary said

That you were Big Ed Walsh, the Hall-of-Famer,
The White Sox great, best pitcher in the world
When giants roamed the diamond. I rode
A summer milk route with a forty-gamer
Who never hinted that he once bestrode
A famous mound and, like a titan, hurled

His smokeball past a batter. I've since gone
Driving through the hills to Cooperstown,
Mr. Walsh, down to the Hall of Fame
To see your plaque upon a wall of stone,
But you were not transfigured by your name —
All I recall is milk that wore a crown.

LETTER TO AN EDITOR

Our Hero conjures up his ancient friend,
The literary Weaver, editor
And correspondent, in his printery
Belowstairs in the house where East Cleveland
Becomes the Heights. He was the guarantor
Of evenings filled with printer's deviltry

And conversation — nights that otherwise
Would have been lost in smog and Erie mist.
        Dear Loring, *he implores,* I've missed you well
These several years. I know that you despise
Shows of emotion. Forgive me. You don't exist,
So I must follow though I go through Hell.

I dream about your office down below;
The flywheel of your press turning around,
The fonts of type, the tubes of murky ink.
Upstairs your fabled wife treads to and fro —
Hart Crane's aunt, billowing like a mound
Of lace and lavender, attempts to think

Of one more bar of music to compose.
Turn off the press — it rumbles to a halt.
We sit and talk among those paneled walls —
Cleveland recedes and starts to decompose.
The strokes of fate are muffled in your vault,
And we can barely hear her siren calls.

I count it as a personal offense,
Loring, when someone dies, someone I know,
Particularly you. What did you get
Out of this retreat? It makes no sense.
How can I calculate the tab I owe
And pay you back? You've buried me in debt.

I must resort to dreams. I turn within
My winding sheets and wait for you to come
To stand beside my stead. You proffer me
A book you've set in leaden type, but on
Those pages there is emptiness. I thumb
The volume through. I read that you are gone.

INTERLUDE:

SLUMBER

*Our Hero is exhausted, and his head
Is reeling from his labors. He glances to
The clock upon the wall. He sees the night
Is far advanced. He switches off the light
And sits in darkness feeling shades of blue —
He has been writing letters to the dead.*

*It's time, he thinks, to rise and go to bed.
He wonders whether he has laid to rest
Any of those ghosts who populate
His dreams — descend the attic stairs and wait
Beside his pillow. He understands their quest;
Therefore, he pens these letters to the dead.*

*He knows that everything was never said
Among them while they thrived; he further knows
That somehow he must say it, or his debt
Will grow until, entangled in its net,
He drowns within the depths of what he owes.
He gathers up his letters to the dead,*

*Shuffles them in darkness. But, instead
Of getting up and going to his room,
He hefts them in his hand. The slender sheaf
Feels as though composed of moss and leaf.
Then, thinking that he smells a grave perfume,
His eyes close on his letters to the dead.*

He dreams his words are waiting to be read.
They lie upon the earth, begin to brown
And crumble into loam. Out of their mold
A herb begins to grow. Its leaves unfold
To drink the night. A bud swells at its crown;
Balm blossoms from the letters to the dead.

When he awakens, an incarnate red
Transfuses the horizon: it is dawn.
The letters, scattered on his morning table,
Show palely forth from under umbral sable —
The shades still linger; they will not be gone —
He must resume his letters to the dead.

THE OBSESSION

Last night I dreamed my father died again,
A decade and a year after he dreamed
Of death himself, pitched forward into night.
His world of waking flickered out and died —
An image on a screen. He is the father
Now of fitful dreams that last and last.

I dreamed again my father died at last.
He stood before me in his flesh again.
I greeted him. I said, "How are you, father?"
But he looked frailer than last time I'd dreamed
We were together, older than when he'd died —
I saw upon his face the look of night.

I dreamed my father died again last night.
He stood before a mirror. He looked his last
Into the glass and kissed it. He saw he'd died.
I put my arms about him once again
To help support him as he fell. I dreamed
I held the final heartburst of my father.

I died again last night: I dreamed my father
Kissed himself in glass, kissed me goodnight
In doing so. But what was it I dreamed
In fact? An injury that seems to last
Without abatement, opening again
And yet again in dream? Who was it died

Again last night? I dreamed my father died,
But it was not he — it was not my father,
Only an image flickering again
Upon the screen of dream out of the night.
How long can this cold image of him last?
Whose is it, his or mine? Who dreams he dreamed?

My father died. Again last night I dreamed
I felt his struggling heart still as he died
Beneath my failing hands. And when at last
He weighed me down, then I laid down my father,
Covered him with silence and with night.
I could not bear it should he come again —

I died again last night, my father dreamed.

REFLECTIONS IN AN ATTIC ROOM
A Sonnet Redoubled

As if one needed to begin to write;
As though one had to have a pen at hand,
Paper smoothening to the touch of night,
Light sifting across the page like wind and sand.

This is the scrivener's fallacy, the hour
Abraded by sand and wind, by willful words:
They scrape at vision, they scarify and scour —
The urn becomes a scattering of shards;

The wind, a voice freed of its hollow shell
Noting nothings echoing in the bone
Bleaching among the dunes of time that swell:
They shift, remembering they once were stone.

Sit stony-eyed; watch the words curl and come
Still-born to life between the joint and thumb.

Dear Father: You are dead. What's there to say?
Yet I'll go on to say it, as you know,
Or may not, as the case may be. Just so,
Our monologues continue on their way,
Two streams of silence rising out of clay,
Passing each other in the essential flow
Of stars and atoms. Watch them rise and go,
Falling in vortices of night and day:

The grass grows green, the suns and planets turn
Upon a field of sable. Brine turns to blood,
I turn to you as day turns into night,
As flesh turns in to earth. I cannot spurn
The flame you gave to me upon the flood
As if one needed to begin. To write

Is useless. "Poetry makes Nothing happen,"
As Auden said. It happens anyhow,
Rising upon the eternal tide of Now,
Engulfing everything — the field, the aspen,
Herb, rock and furrow. So we sigh, grasp pen,
Ink and paper, then we sit down to plow
Another row of letters. We endow
The meadow with another seed to open.

And when it does, what will the blossom be?
Another flower in a sea of flowers?
A blooming and a withering of the land
That once was ocean, that once more shall be sea
Rising to blood again to invest these hours
As though one had to have a pen in hand?

Here in an attic study rising to
A peak in the winter dark, one thinks at times
Of love; one thinks of synonyms and rhymes
That come as close as words are wont to do
To what it once was like when the flesh was new
And closed with flesh in torrid zones and climes.
What was it like? Whose were those pantomimes
Between the sheets that got the rave reviews?

Those sheets — those wrinkled sheets: they press in close
Upon recall. The books that line these shelves
Are filled with love songs yellowing and trite:
Verbena pressed between the leaves verbose.
Our sheets untwine, leaving to our selves
Paper smoothening to the touch of night.

The attic listens to the scratching pen.
Outdoors, the wind has sunk. The snow is deep,
The neighbors in their steads are fast asleep,
Dreaming of when they will awake again.
Nothing is happening, nor will it when
They lift their lids to look into the deep
Trance of wakening. The ink will keep
The stillness that inhabits books and men,

Will keep it and disgorge it as the leaf
Turns, veined and sere, and then begins to brown
Under the rooftree, beneath the moving hand.
The words accumulate, become a sheaf
Of seasons as the silence filters down,
Light sifting across the page like wind and sand.

Imagine this: a battering at the door;
The voice of anguish pleading, "Give us curds,
Crusts, crumbs of meaning — pray you, give us words!
We need the Secret Name, and so much more —
A sense of purpose from your ample store
Of synonyms and antonyms! Rewards
Undreamt await if you extend towards
Your fellow man a portion of your lore!"

But the knocker lies against the stolid wood,
The panel does not echo. The empty hall
Contains but peeling paper and a sour
Smell of waiting. It must be understood
There is no understanding, only gall:
This is the scrivener's fallacy. The hour

Is late. The atmosphere is thick. The earth
Is running down. The fishes in the sea
Are drowned in silt. Each blade of grass, each tree
Is blighted. There has been a monstrous birth,
And plenitude has been transformed to dearth —
The Magi slouch away from Galilee.
"The pen is mightier than the sword," but see
It beaten into shares of slender worth:

It settles in its rut and plows its row.
The poisonous sun and parching raindrops slough
From brow and temple. Emaciated birds,
Before the wrinkled seed can sprout and grow,
Seize it for ivied towers wearing down,
Abraded by sand and wind, by willful words.

Go, little book, and bear thy wordy freight
Away from me as fast as e'er thou may —
I'm sick to death of everything you say.
I wrote you out in sundry hours late
When I long since ought to have hit the hay —
But did I seek sweet dreaming? Did I sate
The wingéd Pegasus on an early date,
In a timely moment? Nay, I say you, neigh!

I entertained the nightmare in my room.
I watched that grim old nag bend to devour
The grain of bitterness, the oats of doom,
The silage of depression. Little, sour
Book, I loathe thy messages of gloom —
They scrape at vision, they scarify and scour.

Build me more stately vessels, O my Soul!
I have a pot to piss in, sure enough,
But I've a fancy for more fancy stuff:
Amphorae full of oils, a wassail bowl,
Kraters of flowers. Ceramics is my goal:
A funerary urn, built good and tough,
Of alabaster so that, when I slough
This clay, my ash won't end up in a hole.

But what is this? I look into my heart
And find a crock chock-full of feeble words;
A thunder-jug beladen with a fart;
Stained paper, and a nest of nestling turds —
And as I watch, the paper falls apart;
The urn becomes a scattering of shards.

I wrote a book called *Curses and Laments*.
There was, it seems, a modicum of scents
In such an exercise, but only that:
A modicum, for it relieves frustration,
But changes nothing else in God's creation.
You pucker up and whistle in your hat;
You break a little wind when you're intense —
I wrote a book called *Curses and Laments*.

You take a certain pleasure in the smell
Of fire and brimstone. They can go to Hell,
Those bastards that have muscled you around.
Leave them a curse and then go underground
To breathe the air where you have loosed to dwell
A wind, a voice freed of its hollow shell.

What will we talk about beneath the stone?
"I have a little dust stuck in my eye."
"Today the worms are restless. I can feel
Them turning." "Pardon me, I have a cold —
I cannot stop my coughin'." "Thought I'd die
Of laughter when my nasty neighbor went
Out in the rain and caught her death." "I saw
Pale Ryder the other day — he's looking old
And out of sorts." "I wait for the telephone
To ring, but my children never seem to call.
Perhaps it's out of order — the reaper-man
Doesn't service the equipment he has sold."
Perhaps it's much like life — we'll merely lie
Noting nothings echoing. In bone-

Yards poets slowly accumulate.
I sometimes wonder if, on Judgment Day,
We'll all rise up in glory to afflate,
Converse, and each recite his latest lai.
Can rime be so perverse? In Plato's State
We'd all be banished — even the great Good Gray
Poet. But where in God's name could we go —
To that grand Writers' Conference Below?

But even there we would, it seems to me,
Be welcomed none too warmly to pause or dwell.
There'd be the Devil to pay, inevitably,
For there are limits to tolerance in Hell.
If we are left alone with our poetry
Bleaching among the dunes of time, that's well.

So Limbo's won and Paradise is lost.
My attic room is filling up with smoke:
I sit and talk with Geoffrey, Will — a host

Of my confreres. We pass the time with joke
And bawdry. There is little else to do —
The centuries lie heavy as a yoke

Upon the roof; the crackling of the glue
In all our bindings shatters this still air.
Our words and verse go whistling up the flue.

We pilgrims to Perdition sit and stare
Into the silence of sere marrow-bone.
I proffer the hemlock cup — they do not dare

Accept, for if they drank I'd be alone.
They shift, remembering they once were stone.

And in my pipe smoke I can just discern
The outlines of a sonnet redoublé,
A skeleton of what is my concern:
The meaning of it all. My smoke is gray.

I ponder carefully these artful rounds
And think about the things I have to say —
I try some lines aloud. The noise redounds
To my House of Fame, and meters ricochet

From the sloping walls to die upon my ears.
Where are the hare of soul, the baying hounds
Of the Apocalypse? Where are the tears
Condensed from feelings language seldom sounds?

My room is silent; my pen is chill and dumb.
Sit stony-eyed with words that curl and come.

Now it is almost done, this foolish thing
That I have penned. The lines have nearly jelled,
And I must ask if I have felt compelled
To write, or merely willed myself to sing

This song that few will ever care to read.
And was I born, or was I merely made,
Concocted of myself — the man of trade,
Not the Bard God conjured out of need

To cure the universe? I do not care.
To be a poet of whatever sort
Will help to pass this journey to the Court
Of Ultimate Decisions. This is fare

I pay and eat — these lines that fall and come
Stillborn to life between the joint and thumb.

LETTER TO MOTHER

Dear Mother, *writes Our Hero*, You won't dread
My writing you this letter to the dead —
Not even if you read it. You'd not recall
A word a moment later. You've built a wall
Between the world and you, a wall of glass
Opaque as pearl, through which no moments pass.

You lie in one position all day long,
Oblivious to silence as to song.
You'd like to die, but you have been betrayed
By your own body. Death has been delayed
Because the flesh is not yet ready to
Give up the ghost — it will not take its cue

And ring the curtain down upon this play
That has no climax — the scene just seeps away.
Imperceptibly the footlights dim,
The heroine held hostage by the whim
Of fate and accident — not even age
Will help you in your exit from the stage.

There is no need for me here to rehearse
The acts in your decline. It seemed perverse
At first, and then I thought you must be ill,
But you were not. It was an act of will,
Wasn't it, Mother? You just gave up, gave in,
Threw up your hands — you lost the wish to win.

But who or what is it you've really killed?
Much of your past, and part of mine is stilled,
Lost to one-half of our common memory.
Time's siling hands have scoured it like emery
From your mind, and I am not your son
In some essential way, I'm not the one

I was when you remembered who I was,
But someone less. This is what dying does:
It murders the survivors, cell by cell,
Until we too fall victim to the fell
And fragile flesh. We owe it to each other
Not to give in until we have to, Mother.

THE DEAD LETTER OFFICE

*Our Hero has been writing to the dead
Because they have been coming to his room
During his sleep and cumbering his dreams.
They never speak, however, and it seems
That if he hopes to send them back to Doom
He must write missives which must then be read.*

*But how can he be sure they will be read?
He addresses them c/o Office of the Dead,
Stamps them all and sends them to their doom.
But have they been delivered, or is there room
For a sure and certain doubt? He sighs. It seems
There's nothing for it but to resort to dreams.*

*He goes to bed and enters into dreams.
He stands before a building made of red
Incendiary brick lost in the seams
Of cobbled streets. Office of the Dead
Is lettered on the door in runes of rheum
And flaking paint, as though the Day of Doom*

*Had cracked upon these boards. "Is this the doom
Of writing, then?" Our Hero asks, "of dreams?"
For he has forced the door, stands in a room
Hollow as any novel he has read,
Empty as any poem, and as dead.
There are no letters here, or so it seems*

At first — but then an envelope that seems
To have been spared for solitary doom
Catches his eye — it is not for the dead;
It is addressed to him. Our Hero dreams
He opens it and reads. What he has read
He understands...but only in that room.

When he awakens in his own bedroom,
He cannot think of what it was he seems
To have understood in the epistle that he read
There in the cobbled streets where he sought the doom
Of letters full of silence, the sound of dreams
Echoing in the Office of the Dead.

ODES AND ELEGIES

THE BIRDSONG BLUES

The graybird sings as though there were no fall,
He chirps and sings as though there were no fall,
No wild west wind or winter snows at all.

The world will end and then where will he be?
The wind will call and then where will he be
With nothing at all for him to do or see?

He'll hover underneath the northern lights,
His wings will hold him still beneath the lights
That flicker and race in wild electric flights

Across the cloud-hung oceans. He will lie
Above the misty oceans — float or lie
With nothing left to note, nowhere to fly.

Till then he sings — he gives his song to air,
To anything that might be listening there.

THE DAME WHO CARRIED HER CANE IN HER COFFIN
A title invented by Wallace Stevens but unused until now.

She was the lady Donovan-O'Neill
Who lived alone with others of her ilk
With divans and damaskas lately seen

And early sought to furnish forth her mind.
It was a nebula of rosaries
That went revolving where she lay among

The candelabra, confections of the wake,
The ductile tears of elders, and the young
Who raised their lace bandannas in alas.

Upon her lids small change winked there at Death
Who stood to gain the least against her will.
Tumblers clinked chorales in umbral tones;

"The sullen diapason of the sea"
Responded in the seashell of her ear;
Silk sang to her, mahogany and teak

Antiqued themselves and her: she was la belle
Of Boston, without ire, who left no heir
Unturned, who never tuned an air

Nor breathed a centime's scandal. There she lay,
Chiffon and velveteen, high-toned and waled
Beyond the stockinged throng while in her grasp

Whence it had fallen from her to la grippe,
Not to be raised anon, her prop and stay
When she'd been able — the good and proper cane

Of dim repute, restored to her in spades.
But not to her, for she was in their minds,
Not in their mist. She'd walked beyond the haze

Of waking into slumber with her wood.
The coffin had dissembled her catarrh,
Her fever dissipated in the flue.

She was no longer she, but sybarite
Of Was, the melancholic dame of Seem
At one with timbre, nevermore of would.

ELEGY ON EIGHT LINES BY CONRAD AIKEN
FROM *A Letter from Li Po*

There is a silence lying on the air
And on the carpet of muted hue and weave
Beneath the desk. Upon the desk there lies
A letter long as time and deep as love.

Whom is the missive from, to whom addressed?
What are these words that one can scarcely say
In the dim room of dream, glimpsed in a flare,
That lightning-stroke which in your dream you saw?

Have I directed these syllables to you,
Or are they yours addressed to me? A glove
Has fallen on a page to contemplate
Dust on the doorsill or an ink-stained sleeve.

The moon pours through the window streaked and cracked,
Flows over a ragged dike of books to lave
The pen of shadow spinning its spider thread,
And with it all its local web of love.

Beyond the window, in the meadow there
Where entropy dissolves the evening chord
Against the sky, the letter comes to life:
The song is in the peach tree and the ear.

The room sinks farther into stillness where
It mulls the meaning of its monotone.
Night has written itself upon the leaves;
The singer holds his phrase, the rising moon

Which scratches its arc among the hieroglyphs
Scrawled upon the dark. What is the word
The world attempts to sing in letters, leaves?
Among the leaves we are the hidden bird;

We are the arching moon, the night descending
Among our limbs throughout long ages starred,
Destined to wither sere and still at last,
And with the falling leaf the falling bird.

THE BLACK DEATH
London, 1665

"I have a buboe, mum," my daughter said
and raised her sleeve to show me. In the street
the bellman cried aloud, "Bring out your dead!"

The heart of me froze like a drop of sleet,
dropped into my bowel when my darling child
raised up her sleeve to show me. In the street

the crier's bell rang out both dark and wild.
The end of time opened like a flower,
fell into my bowel as my darling child

showed me her fatal wound. Our final hour
blossomed before my eyes in Satan's garden,
for the end of time had opened like a flower.

I felt the heart in me begin to harden
against a Deity who could ordain
such an evil blossoming of Satan's garden.

What were the sins that could have earned such bane?
What sort of Deity could so ordain?
 "I have a buboe, mum," my daughter said.
The bellman cried aloud, "Bring out your dead!"

THE NIGHT BEFORE THE BATTLE, 1865
A painting by James Henry Beard

The men are sleeping on the battlement.
One man reclines against a broken cannon,
Old Glory in his arms, her brilliant skirts
Lying across his thigh. He is content,
One may assume. It's hard to see the others
Scattered among the shadows strewn like stone
Across the night, although the moonlight flirts
With the outlines of this rallying of Brothers-

In-Arms. One must look close to count those who
Are most obscure. Some seem to disappear
Nearly to nothing. "Nearly" is not the word,
For one can just perceive the stone wall through
The body of this man who sits, his poll
Resting upon his knees — some gathered here
Are phantom sleepers who will once more gird
Their loins and hearts in answer to the call

That dawn will bring ringing along the pall
Of mist beneath the moon flooding the fields
Below with the cold immensity of dream.
Two are awake: one of them, on the wall,
Stands lookout dressed like Banquo's ghost
And stares into the night. What power he wields
With his ancient eye is moot, for its piercing beam
Is turned away from us. He stands his post

Listening, but does the other sentinel
See and hear more clearly? — he sights along
The barrel of a cannon aiming out
Into the umber brooding within the well
Of stillness beneath the moon. His empty sockets
Stare at nothingness. He hears the song
Of death echoing in his skull, the shout
Of the charging shades and of the bursting rockets —

Soon his comrades must rise up in a host
And, like his own, their moonlit dreams be lost.

BLUES FOR GEORGE GERSHWIN, 1898-1937

When I was three you stepped out of the light.
When I was three years old you spurned the light
And wandered off into the dark of night.

You left behind a melody or two,
A tune, a song, a melody or two,
And that was quite enough for you to do

To justify your stay among us here,
To pay your way while you were with us here
Upon this mortal coil, this spinning sphere.

When I grew up I heard the songs you made,
I listened, and I learned the songs you made
And wished — oh! how I wished that you had stayed.

I do not understand why you were taken
So young. Some force of Nature was mistaken
When it decided to leave the world forsaken

Of all that possibility of song,
That minstrel's bag of melody and song
That now we'll never hear forever long.

Therefore we pick your bones and make up tunes
Out of the scraps you left, those scraps of tunes
Your brother Ira kept through nights and noons

Until he got too old and joined you there
Wherever you are, rose up and joined you there
To help you strike those strings in the ringing air.

DISTANT SOUND
In memory of Philip Houdlette

A line of lightning clouds the distant sound
Of thunderweather moving like the air
Among the trees. Along the river where
The tide is siling downstream may be found
Great blue herons standing on middleground
Listening for food. Swimming there
A rock pretends to be a turtle, square
Of beak and will, averse to being drowned.

And if these things are seldom what they seem
And never what they are, then why should we
Believe in them, or not believe? In dream
Morning turns to lightning on the tree
Moving beside the river where the gleam
Of evening rides the current to the sea.

THE GREAT ICE STORM OF 'NINETY-EIGHT

The rains have stopped, and now the woods are crystal,
The roads are silver rivers sluicing through
This January air. We hear reports
Out of the forest that tell us boles are splitting,
Branches breaking, birches and maples spitting
Showers of ice. Now and then a pistol
Cracks. Nearby, a power line resorts
To sparks and even flame—gold, red and blue.

It would appear a giant has stepped upon
The upper boughs of all the trees in sight.
Darkness falls as solidly as the rain
Upon the lampglow showing in silent houses
Along these country roads, but nothing rouses
Anything to action. A nearby pond
Lies dully in its hollow, hardly frozen.
If there were streetlamps its water would drink their light.

The hours drag themselves through night. At last
Life begins once more and day by day
Men commence to mend the devastation,
But slowly, slowly. It will be weeks before
Maine is tamed again. Who will restore
Our confidence in our civilizing power
After this rain of glass? The storm is past,
For now — another broods on the horizon.
Winter will linger, and its runes are gray.

HERB PLAYS WITH THE BLUES
Wednesday, 12 September 2001

Alas, my buddy Herb has got the blues,
My poor old buddy Herb's deep in the blues.
But it's an exercise, it's not the news

That's got him in the dumps. It's not the dust
That's covered New York City deep in dust
And rubble — no, it's not the boom and bust

Of terror from the skies on a summer day,
A brilliant, clear and sunny summer day
Buried in suffocating clouds of gray

Smoke and soot and scattered body parts
Of once whole people merely body parts
That now must be removed in trucks and carts

From the streets of Old New York. Our world is changed
Forever now by monsters, forever changed,
And we who live in it have been estranged

From what was real. The solid earth we knew,
That solid sod that once we walked and knew
Is now surreal — planes dropping from the blue

Into towers falling onto streets
That are no longer avenues and streets
But silent canyons. Herb, this form repeats,

This form called blues, but so too does despair,
These images of death and of despair
That sunder us beyond hope of repair.

AFTER SCHOOL
A Samsong, A Form Invented by R. S. Gwynn

Here is a boy just out of school.

Here is that same boy now at large.
Here is the officer in charge.

Here is the bunker where they lie
Here in the desert sere and dry
Under the hot sun in the sky.

There is the liar with his prattle
Moving the boys around like cattle.
Listen, you'll hear his sabre rattle.
There is the man who began the battle.

There is the coward who, when young,
Raised his finger, stuck out his tongue
At the flag, emptied his lung
Of a hawker when the bell was rung,
Calling the boys whom he stood among.

There's the commander now in chief.
There is the robber baron, the thief
Wrapped in religion and his belief
That this is his land, his personal feoff.
The ship of State is upon the reef.
Here are the mothers lost in grief.

Here is the blood. Here is the oil.
Here are bitterness and turmoil,
Here the men and boys who were loyal;
Here is death upon foreign soil —
There is the man who believes he's royal

Delivering a medal, a star
Of gold on a flag. "Well, there you are,
Mrs. Jones. Have a cigar.
Be proud of your son. Tell him au revoir —

"Sometimes life can be too cruel.
Beneath these sands, though, there's a pool
Of liquid gold, and we need the fuel."

Here is a body in the sun.
Here is a life that is undone.

Here lies a boy just out of school.

THE DAY WE BOMBED THE MOON
(AND BARACK OBAMA WON
THE NOBEL PEACE PRIZE),
A SESTINA

October ninth, 2009, we sent
A rocket off to Luna. We meant to bomb her
Into submission? No, our good intent:
To blow up surface dust to test for ice.
On the same day the Nobel Prize Committee
Amazed the world by bestowing its amity

Award upon a tyro. A calamity,
It seemed to some — an evil precedent
Imposed upon America by committee.
They gave the Peace Prize to Barack Obama!
Many Republicans needed to ask for ice-
Water and Schnapps, or even an oxygen tent.

No one had dreamed an explosion of this extent
Could blow moondust in the face of amity
Around the House and Senate. It wasn't nice
That those Norse should cause old pols to resent
Explosive love. It was a suicide bomber
NASA sent to ruin comity —

If not around the world, the R. N. C.
At the very least. Gaddafi in his tent
Celebrated Luna's death. "Embalm her!"
Was his battle cry, his enmity
For global infidelity was sent
To Cocoa, Florida, well-packed in ice.

But NASA said, "It isn't very nice
To imply we had an impact on the Committee
Rather than the moon! Our bomb was sent
Out into space. We're not incompetent!"
Meanwhile, a wave of pure tsunamity
Engulfed the Oval Office, and Obama,

Although surprised himself, felt like the balm or
Salve of sweet salvation in a trice
Had rehabilitated amity,
Restored a modicum of comity
To the world at large to some extent,
One could sense the very aloe's scent.

Barack Obama, the Nobel Committee,
And malcontents hope NASA finds its ice,
But what price amity amid dissent?

COLUMBIAN ODE

Strophe.

When Columbia broke up in the skies over the western states
February the first, 2003, everyone watched the tape
Loop repeatedly. We sat in the web spun by the spider once
More, as often we'd done since the defunct century flushed itself
Down historical tubes: maybe we knew nothing would come to pass
After all in our dim consciousness. What happens when we expect
Something, usually? Not much. It's the bad joke of the Laughing God
Who will wait while the Earth spins in the dark spaces between his toes
Till the moment we least look for any tragedy. Then he hits
Hard. We think that we've grown — harder than nails, shields
                                        that surround our souls!
What a joke! We are knocked flat on our broad backs and
                                              discover once
More how vulnerable Man is to Fate's blows. We are fragile still.

Antistrophe.

No song is sung or elegy spoken as
Great sorrow settles over a tragedy,
   Falls into chasms opened into
      Misery. How shall we find our mourning's

True voice in keening, hopeless despair, or in
Wounds newly suffered — coins to be squandered on
   Grief governed not by thought but feelings?
      Time is required for grief to ripen

Into melody, into sorrow's music.

Epode.

Into melody, into sorrow's music
There will quietly steal another lyric
After all of the requiems have ended,
After most of the mourners have departed.
It will be but a bar or two of heartbeat
Just at first, but a murmur in the bloodstream
Building finally to a constant drumming
Running through the aorta to the fingers,
To the toe-tips and belly. It will be like
Springtime touching the edges of a frozen
Mountain rivulet which, in its descending
Over gradients of downland, brings renewal
To the valleys below. The world begins to
Stir again and the eyes begin to open
Onto vapors arising over waters
Lying under the glimmering of daylight.

LINES TO BE ETCHED ON A WINDOW
For Donald Justice

Clearly, you may see clear through me,
As though I were not here.

TSUNAMI

The world was washed away by a wall of water
That first became the horizon: a rising wall
That pulled the shallows outward and away
From the shores. The coastal sealife washed
Out to sea with the boats. For a moment there was
Stillness everywhere, and then the world

Listened to a roar that became the world,
The sound of a thousand thunders, not of water
Merely, but of the fluid earth. It was
Then that liquid turned to stone, a wall
Hard as rock screaming that before it washed
Ashore and tore the rose child away

From the whipped, lifted the torsos, mother him away
From the ocean he worked. The place became the world,
Crushed the beaches along the buildings, washed
Limbs and father into the trees. The gristmill water
Filled the wells with salt and gristmill. A wall
Of bricks became a blood grinding what was

Paste behind it into a lying. It was
Mud and plants and trees spun away
Into a nothing of single eddies now all
Things, backwashes and polluted and whirled
In items of undifferentiated water
Where everything maelstrom could be washed.

What could float, buried, what could be washed
Away was unsafe away, out to sea, was
Washed in a tree that held, held above water
Or drowned or floated in mud or floated away
Into who knew where? It was a world
That was caught ashore, but at sea the wall

Did not exist. It was safe above the wall,
On the surface of the wave that rose and washed
Away the earthen world, the solid world,
The world where creatures breathed an air that was
Lighter than liquid. It sent them far away
From breath, from sight, from the living world.

Instead, it gave them a whelming wall that was
Scoured into the minds of those not washed away
From the world of earth into the world of water.

RUSSET OAK

Autumn has fallen out of the russet oak
And whispers along the ground pulling a cloak
Of silence in its wake. If it has a tale
To tell it may be in the haze of smoke

That hovers in the air over the vale
Where the Eastern River cuts a shallow trail
Through the reeds. The house is full of shades
Of gray and dust these days. The sun is pale

In the staring windows, and the carpet fades
In icy increments as the brook cascades
Into the tidal river beneath Blinn's Hill.
November will soon descend in white glissades

To try the water with a touch and fill
Its book of leaves with hieroglyphs a quill
Will trace among the reeds. Perhaps the folk
Of yesteryear may one day return and spill

Their broken silence into the hazy smoke
That fills a summer surrounding this russet oak.

YEATS' BIRTHDAY
Friday, June 13, 2008

The sunshine shines upon Sligo's son this morn,
For 'tis the birthday of the Bard of bards.
William lies sleeping in a bed of reeds
On Innisfree where the white swan preens and feeds,
Where the honeybee in the loud glade guards
The silence to be found in gorse and thorn.
May he one day awaken and sing again
Of the good green land of bracken, brae and glen,

Oh may he sing once more of the lovely light
That lies upon the meads of Ireland,
May he tell us tales once more of night
Turned into clarity. Let the sun demand
The swan be as a flame of snowy white
Burning out of the sconce of sea and sand.

SEASONS DOWN EAST

Summer Time

Summer time winds down its waterfall,
Wends a dwindling way toward the fall.
Along these banks ghosts of crocus sing —
Choruses of sunlight fall and sing.

This craft of hours drifts among the reeds —
Goes with the flow among the shaking reeds,
The silver alders — carries on in time
Of bitter-root and aloes, vetch and thyme.

In the eddies smoky heron stand;
Silting waters pool their current, stand
Where muskrats slide. Mossback turtles sun
In silence, just below the rim of sun
Cast here by cedar looming on the shore.

The shuttle of this umber of the shore
Is slower than the hovering of trout
Among the rocks — the stony skin of trout
Maintaining equilibrium in the flow
Of earth and water, the incandescent flow
Of fire and air encircling the tides —
Flood, neap-of-the-moon, and ebb. The turning tides
Break in the estuaries, on the sand.
They dwell below these falls, the shiftless sand.

Autumn Time

Here in the course of waters there decline,
Through foliage and shadow in glissade,
The brooks that feed an autumn's cataract —
Closing a season, veiling the light's descent.

Leafmold recollects the avalanche
A year ago, a century — the lapse
Felt in the trunk, the bone. The precipice
Leans outward, listens to the gorge, and drops
A shard of red or brown, threatens to topple
Into the chasm, but hesitates. The plunge
Of gulls and bitterns on the wheel of fall
Follows the combers that rock the coast and settle
Under the floating leaves, the grains that sile.

Winter Time

Beneath its crust of hoar the water moves
Deep in the bluing lumen of the moon —
Not darkly, though the sunken stones are dark,
But not in light, even when the sun
Casts down its weightfulness of chill and flare.

The redbird on the riverbank stops cold,
And in the cedar boughs a jay reflects
Among thin stalactites of ice whose green
And fluid silver pierces to the quick
The squirrel's eyes. The waterfall has made
Caves and spires of solid froth to mark
The entrance to the grotto of the sea:

Floes wash there, beyond the petrified
Salt-marsh reeds and grasses. A single seal
Stamps the ice with life, diminishes
As the sky impends, blending gray with gray,
Even the waves lost to the horizon.

Spring Time

The rage! The rage! The quick good-natured rage
Of waters in the gorge, the rapids splaying
Hours beneath the fall, the drop of time
And spume of moment — coursing up the stream
Salmon flash trajectories from the sea:
Ten thousand arcs and bows beneath the sun
Split to prisms on the roaring stones.

CAUTIONARY POEMS

FATHERS

1. *First Father*

I see him standing on the empty plain
As dawn begins to break across his eyes.
He is alone, this first of all my fathers,
But he can sense his scions and his daughters
Following down the looming centuries,
For time has started weaving through his brain,
And he can think. He understands at last
What must become, and what's become his past.

And here I stand upon this farthest link
Staring down the line of molecules
Twisted in a spiral arc. I gaze
The other way to where the whirling haze
Rises over dark and depthless pools
And wonder what the final man must think.

2. *Fathers of the Tribe*

His sons and grandsons travel with the tribe
As it drifts out of the immense savannah
Following the herds, but searching for
Something else as well. They *must* explore,
Apparently. For Eden? For Nirvana?
Their leaders are unable to describe
What they are seeking past these eastern sands,
Moving always northward to colder lands.

What have we found beyond those roaming droves
That led us into canyons made of glass?
Where do we go from here? How shall we feed
The starving myriads whose simplest need
No longer can be met on earth? En masse
We need again a miracle of loaves.

3. *The Final Father*

And as they stop, wherever they may move,
Each scion takes his mate who bears his seed,
The generations of First Father's loins.
Time spends these children like so many coins
Minted from the soil. The earth has need
Of purses full of these. The parents rove
Into the mystery to make it known,
To turn the strangest climes into their own.

Now we are everywhere. The human race
Has filled the niches that the world provided.
What's left is Easter Island duplicated
On a massive scale. We are checkmated
By ourselves; we are the tribe divided
Staring hopelessly to outer space.

A PATERNAL CURSE

My father used to shout at me
When I'd again done something wrong,
And bite his hand and tear his hair —
All I could do was stand and stare
At this berserker gone headlong
Into madness of the nth degree:
 "I curse the day that I was born!"

A strange thing for a preacher of
An odd Italian stripe to say
To me. Did I request a shove
Into life myself? Oh, no!
If I'd been asked I'd never go
To hear him sing his song of love:
 "I curse the day that I was born!"

But I did love him anyway —
A sweeter man I've never known.
At every meal I'd hear him pray
For peace and happiness for all.
He hoped that I would hear the call
Myself, but no: I'd heard him bray,
 "I curse the day that I was born!"

I soon discovered what he meant.
I watched the world as it was torn
Limb from limb, its substance rent
To shards with swords and teeth and claws.
The proposition gave me pause
To ponder existence's intent
And curse the day that I was born!

PASSING THE TIME

Where am I going? How do I know where?
Why do I write as I saunter along,
passing the time on the road to nowhere?

I'm humming a tune, mumbling a song
to kill as much time as I sensibly can —
that's why I write as I wander along

making the syllables skip and scan,
making the language dance and go deep
to kill as much time as I sensibly can —

to liven the senses before I sleep,
slipping into that ultimate slumber.
Making the language dance and go deep

by counting these syllables without number
and *making* them count is my chosen role.
Slipping into the final slumber

is, of course, my ultimate goal.
Where am I going? How can I know where?
Making time count is my chosen role
while passing time on this road to nowhere.

DOUBLE VISION
A Double Sestina

I.

It came upon me while I was on the crapper
of my father's parsonage, my eyes
boring into the porcelain of the tiles
before me on the wall. The tiles were white.
They spread across the vacancy of time
That seeped into my mind and filled that blank

jug of puberty with a vast Mont Blanc
of sorrow and ennui. On that crapper
I saw that I would have to fill up time
with something more than the nothing that met my eyes,
the emptiness that seeped out of those white
ranges of porcelain whose trackless tiles

led finally to death. I feared those tiles
worse than I feared my death, that ultimate blank-
ness waiting for me on the snowy white
crest of age. I saw life was a crapper
that had to be filled with something. If I closed my eyes
perhaps I could dream myself to a better time

than this one snowing before me. There was no time
to dream. What could I do? I could fill tiles
with words. I could write. I filled my eyes
with reading every day; I could fill blank
sheets with my own words. I rose off that crapper
thinking I might pave my way with white

sheaves laden with stories, poems — I could write
my way to death by filling my living tome
with endless lines of type till I came-a-cropper
at last and alas! perhaps, on the devil's tines,
if I kept my gaze steady and didn't blink,
and if I did not try to romanticize

my life with gods and demons, with the sighs
of wishful thinking, with the little white
lies of religion that covered up the blank
of existence with the stuff that fills a crapper.
I pulled myself out of the abyss of tiles
Ready to take on life and move in time.

I'd use my eyes to read. Perhaps in time
I'd use those words to write, to fill up tiles
With something more than blankness on that crapper.

II.

So that is what I've done. I've been the croupier
in life's casino to this point, with ice
in my arteries. My column of tales
and songs has risen to a decent height
and I am old at last, although not tame
as maybe I should be. But I won't blink

at this point, for why should I wish to blink?
I've been raking in what a good croupier
rakes in — coin of the realm like leaves of thyme,
minutes and moments that one can use to spice
the pot of emptiness when it gains heat
enough to flavor these mortal tales

that I've been cooking up. There's nothing stales
a blend of blandishments quick as a blink
faster than losing interest at its height
even as one's flesh grows crepier
with every year and hour. So, throw some ice
into the mix, perhaps, but never tame

the cold gazpacho one swallows nigh the tomb.
Trade the rake for a ladle, but keep those tales
swirling about in that bucket of mordant ice
and, before your readers can even blink,
serve it like a waiter, not a croupier,
when the flavor has hit its tasteful height.

Some folk feel that life is just a hoot,
a game of chance played with a friendly team
and not alone with "God" as one's croupier
dressed in cummerbund and a set of tails
spinning the wheel. Before you can even blink,
the game is done and you are soused with ice

dumped on you by the "team." You make your choice,
and if you manage to gain a little height
you place your bet, the wheel whirrs — if you blink
(or even if you don't) the suave croupier
pushes over your pile of songs and tales
and you find out there is no game or team,

there's only ice that chills you till you're tame
and lowered by that croupier from about man's height —
he doesn't blink and he will tell no tales.

SESTINA

It drives you crazy to write a sestina.
First off, in order to write a sestina
you need six end-words that don't shout, "Sestina!"
One should hide the fact that it's a sestina
you're writing. I mean, why holler "Sestina!"
if you don't have to? Why give the sestina

game away right away? For a sestina
needs to be a subtle thing. A sestina
should lead readers away from the sestina,
make them think, "This is no kind of sestina,
it's a sixteener, maybe, no sestina
sustaining itself on sestets. Sestina

indeed! I don't believe it. A sestina
doesn't announce itself, "I'm a sestina,
no less! I live on end-words, a sestina
to end sestinas! I'm a sustainer
of sounds, echoes of a choral Sistiner
bouncing off Michaelangelo sixteen or

so ways from Rome to Nome." A fine sestina
that would be. Thirty-nine lines of sestina
mumbling into the reader's ear, "Sestina,
sestina, sestina." Who could sustain a
poem like that for so long? A sestina
ought perhaps to read more like a sonetto

rispetto than like what it is. Sestina
end-words are *teleutons*, and a sestina
should tell you tons about what a sestina
is all about. Certainly, a sestina
is about disguise, subtlety, sestina
reticence, reluctance to be sestina-

like. Rather, it ought to be a soul-stainer,
nuanced, a mind-mellower. A sestina
ought not to be the thing, just the sustainer
of thingness in the memory. Sestina
is teleutonals, not end-words. Sestina
is an earful of sense, not a sestina

ending in a coda that says *sestina,*
repeating end-words, *sestina, sestina,
sestina,* and a final time, *sestina!*

A CAUTIONARY POEM

Be careful in your love. The lips are sweet,
But two may be twice lonelier than one.
Distance is relative. Flesh presses flesh,
Yet atoms spin like suns and planets in
The blood. How close is close? A galaxy
Might turn between you mingled in your sheets.
Where are you as you love? There in your mind
Awash alone in pleasure. Washed ashore
By tide and instinct, the creature lays its eggs
And is swept out to sea again. And then,
Oh, then the cycle starts itself again.
Break it! Say that it stops right here. No more
This futile round willed by the round itself —
Not by you nor any of your kind,
But by the molecules that build their chains
To bind you to the orbits of the blood.
The link splits here. This consciousness assumed
By marrowbone and time need not assume
It must produce another lonely lover,
Another space among the distances.
Be careful what you love, for lips are sweet.

ANOTHER CAUTIONARY POEM

Keep track of trust. Best put it in the bank,
For should you lend it out, if it comes back
It will be damaged goods, a golden coin
With toothmarks on the rim, the edges filed,
The head of Caesar worn by many hands
Till Caesar is effaced, his laurel crown
Reduced to memory, to myth, to dust —
That dust from which the coin was minted fresh.
If it comes back. The chances are it won't.
One might as well turn usurer of love,
Broker of joy, as hope that trust will bring
A dividend or decent interest rate.
He who is rich in trust will die a pauper.
Best put it in the bank. No, not the bank —
A shoebox in the closet; a coffee can
Buried in the flour canister
With double locks upon the cupboard doors.

YET ANOTHER CAUTIONARY POEM

Never say, "Die"! But then, of course, we die.
Then why not say it? "Die!" There — it's been said,
And what's been changed? What has been given up?
A word, no more — a word like other words,
And in a word, what's in a word? One should
Never say "never," perhaps, but if we did
(or didn't, as the case may be), what happens
To that phrase? It won't exist, so then
We wouldn't say it: another concept dead.

A paradox, you say? What good is that?
If words are not precisions, what are they?
Either a thing is so or it is not;
It should not be a knot that twists itself,
Turns in upon itself in subtle ways,
Breaks fingernails, makes thought a labyrinth
Of volute fibers that conduct the mind
To where the Minotaur waits in its mine
Beneath the Cretan surface. Then, "(blank) say 'die!"
"(Blank) say (blank)." Be positive, be firm!
(Blank) is a word that (blank) should pass our lips,
For (blank)ness is a word not true to life —
Though it looks tempting sometimes, (blank)-the-less.

BLOOMSDAY

Today the prodigal returns once more
To roam the cobbled streets of Dublin town,
Returns to raise a toast, to blow the foam
From the glass of his ancestral home,
To quaff its best and take its lifeblood down
Where it will do some good. He will ignore
The little minds, the folk who drove him out
When he was nothing more than a youngling lout,

For now he is their hero, nothing less,
And they will celebrate again this day
The fellow with a pen who, in distress,
Left Ireland to wend an exile's way
Until he could see clear the winding track
That he might take to find the true way back.

FOND POEM
A triolet

Believe me, I am very fond of you;
I think of you with affection in my heart.
My feelings are as strong as they are true,
believe me. I am very fond of you,
but, sad to say, I'm afraid I do not love you;
therefore, my dear, I feel that we must part.
Believe me, I am very fond of you,
I think of you with affection in my heart.

CURRENCY: A SONNENIZIO

"The marvelous current of forgotten things,"
William Wordsworth, *Artegal and Elidure*.

The marvelous current of forgotten things
Drains down Styx till it is no longer current.
We remember a currant or a raisin,
Currently, of our former youthful love life:
Half-baked, doughy, a largely fruitless courante
Danced upon the car seat of a jalopy.
Yes, of course, we wished it to last forever –
Or a thousand years at least of intercourse.
Our first lass, alas! is precursor only,
Never a courtesan for eternities.
Therefore currently we try to remember
What once the world was like riding that current
Now that we've wasted all of youth's currencies
And such occasions are non-occurrences.

STILE
After Ronsard and Yeats

Now you are ancient as the night is old
And firelight flickers on the page before you,
Remember how I tried hard to ignore you
When we were young and I was none too bold?

But I succumbed at last, and now we sit
In wrinkled flesh held up by aching bones
Enjoying one another in monotones
That have been scoured of any touch of wit.

So much for love that stays a little while
Till silence falls and opens up the door
Where shadows gather by the flickering score
To hand us each across the final stile

Allowing us over into the mists that sweep
Across the tumuli in the field of sleep.

SWEET JEAN

Your birthday's rolled around again,
   Jean, sweet Jean,
And I can still remember when
A robe of years had not yet weighed
Upon the figure that I prayed
Might be the instrument I played
     Upon. I did not know
I was the prey, you aimed the bow
   Jean, sweet Jean.

We caught each-other, that's the truth,
   Jean, sweet Jean.
We made a bargain: youth for youth,
And we have been together now
Too many years to wonder how
Many more time will allow.
     All we can do is pray
That it will grant another day,
   Jean, sweet Jean.

Someday one will be left behind,
   Jean, sweet Jean,
To search the hours perhaps to find
That he or she just cannot bear
To walk a barren thoroughfare
Into the mists of who knows where
     Without the other one
Only to find we are undone,
   Jean, sweet Jean.

EPILOGUE

THE BONEYARD BLUES

I.
I'm sitting in the boneyard singing songs,
Sitting singing songs as blue as blue —
Considering my days, their shorts and longs,

The days we spent together, me and you.
Yes, you and me and all those other folks
Who've come and gone. Oh, please don't misconstrue

My meaning — yesterday is gone in strokes,
In strokes and chimes, and time cannot be turned,
I'm well aware; it plays its dirty jokes

And leaves us on our ashes, bare and burned.
We bare our hearts, and then we burn our spans,
But who's to say what lessons we have learned?

The ifs and maybes, shall-bes, will-bes, cans
Turn into bonedust, rusting pots and pans.

II.
Rusting pots and pans pile up and ring,
Pile up and ring us round with shards of loss,
With echoes of the songs we used to sing

In living rooms and bedrooms filled with moss,
With moss and lichen now of recollection.
The kitchen where we used to sit and toss

Together meals of love and of affection
Has grown a mold upon the oven grate,
And there is nothing left of our confection

Except a little sweeting on a plate,
The plate of dreams, its edges chipped and cracked.
In the beginning already it was too late —

The gun was loaded and the deck was stacked.
The tune could not provide what the lyrics lacked.

III.
And so I'm sitting in this boneyard, blue
As blue, and singing songs that leave me cold.
The words — they may be false, they may be true,

They may be new — more likely they are old,
As old as flesh and time. I hear the knell
Of generations as the peals are rolled

Among the stones, within the stony well —
That stone-cold well of destiny gone dry.
Who is the sexton hauling on the bell?

Why is the deacon grinning at us? Why?
Why are his cheekbones sunken, and his teeth
So moonlight-gleaming? Wherefore is his eye

The hollow of a heartbeat underneath
The zero of a withered floral wreath?

Envoi

Just let me drop this note into the dark,
Yes, let me drop this note into the dark —
I'll light it with a match and watch it spark.

I'll sail it into night with fire and flare,
Fly it into darkness, see it flare
And wink out in those shadows circling there.

I'll watch it take its place among the stars,
Among the minor planets and the stars.
I'll hum the blues, not much — a couple bars —

Until the spark has died to inky ash,
And words have flickered into smoken ash.
Then I'll have me a sip of sour mash,

And lean against this marker made of stone
That will not last as long as ink or bone.

Photo of Wesli Court,
a.k.a. Lewis Turco,
by James Russell

'WESLI COURT' is the anagram pen-name under which Lewis Turco writes his traditionally formal poems.

www.ingramcontent.com/pod-product-compliance
Lightning Source LLC
LaVergne TN
LVHW011424080426
835512LV00005B/247